# THE ILLUSTRATED MOTORCYCLE LEGENDS

# HARLEY-DAVIDSON

# ROY BACON

CHARTWELL
BOOKS, INC.

**Previous page: The V-twin Harley-Davidson in its magnificent touring form – right for the job as always.**

Acknowledgements

The author wishes to give special thanks to Dr Martin Jack Rosenblum, historian in the Harley-Davidson archives at Juneau Avenue, Milwaukee, Wisconsin, for his kind assistance and support for this publication. The author and publishers would also like to acknowledge their debt to all who loaned material and photographs for this book. The author would particularly like to thank all his old friends, who rallied round to help and all the new ones made along the way. Much of the older material came from the National Motor Museum at Beaulieu, the Vintage Motor Cycle Club, the archives of EMAP, who hold the old *Motor Cycle Weekly* files, and *Motor Cycle News*, courtesy of the editor. Old and new friends include Don Emde in California, Ian Kerr, Kevin O'Brien, Judy Miedwig in York, Pa – where they build them – who owns that lovely model K, and Alastair McQuaid for photos of an early Sportster and an Iron XR. Our thanks to all.

ISBN 0 7858 0253 3

Designed by Anthony Cohen

Printed and bound in China

# CONTENTS

# FIRM FOUNDATIONS

H arley-Davidson - a legend, a firm which has built just one form of motorcycle for all except its earliest days, whose competitors deride that form - but envy the customer loyalty enjoyed by Milwaukee. In house, it is 'The Motor Company', no need for a name, just as British stamps carry the Queen's head alone, a small conceit but adopted with pride and reason.

For who else has been in the business for 90 years, who else has seen off the competition from home and abroad, who else sees the firm's name and emblem tattooed on arm or body, and who else commands such respect from friend or foe?

It was 1903 when William S. Harley and Arthur Davidson of Milwaukee, Wisconsin, produced their first motorcycle, soon followed by a second, larger machine. In 1904 two production machines followed, Walter Davidson joined his brother and their father built a small wooden shed (10 x 15ft) which was the start of the factory.

Harley-Davidson is famed for its V-twins but the first models had single-cylinder engines installed in a loop frame fitted with bicycle-style forks and direct belt drive. The engine had the inlet valve above the exhaust (ioe), a type known as the F-head, and opening automatically at first. Quite soon a cam, pushrod and rocker were added to make it mechanical. Ignition at first was a crude battery system but a magneto option was introduced in 1909.

From the start the Harley-Davidson was built strong to be reliable at a time when contemporaries were based on bicycle parts and unable to cope with the roads and

**Harley-Davidson began in 1903 with a single, the twin came once William and Arthur were established.**

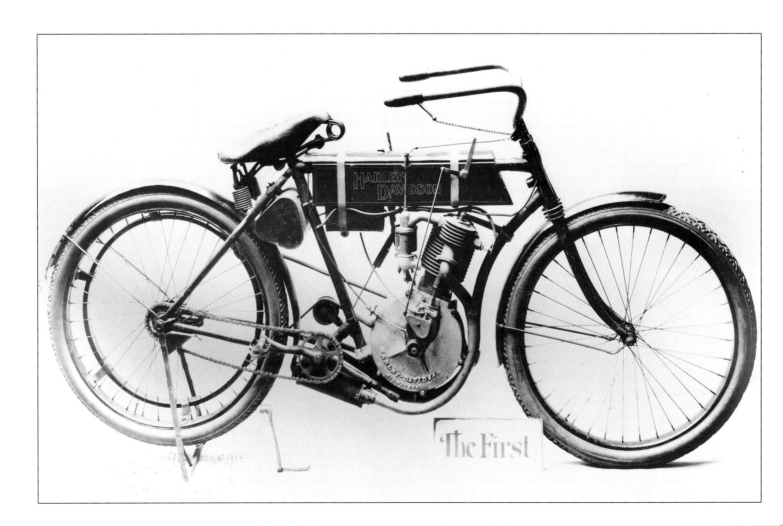

tracks of the times. It was a policy that worked and production rose to 50 in 1906, trebled for 1907, trebled again the next year and soon rose to thousands. By 1906 their colour and good muffler led to the nickname 'The Silent Gray Fellow'.

William A. Davidson joined his two younger brothers in 1907, when leading link forks appeared, Walter won a major endurance run in 1908, and 1909 brought the engine that was to remain the Harley trademark down the years - the V-twin. As with all to follow, its cylinders were at 45 degrees which fitted neatly into the frame.

**Walter Davidson with the machine he used to win a major endurance event in 1908.**

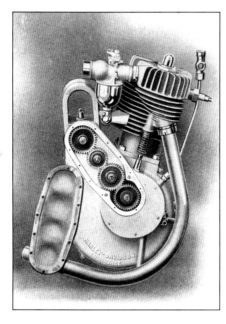

Early singles had an automatic inlet valve. The magneto option was introduced in 1909, its gear train just right for a second cam for the inlet.

This 1907 single fetched a world-record bid of $140,000 when auctioned during 1993.

A 1909-10 single in the 1987 Brighton run, complete with white-wall tyres and many original fittings.

# FIRST TWIN

The first Harley-Davidson twin was not a success, so it was dropped, only to return in 1911, never to look back. It kept the F-head design of the singles, but with a mechanical inlet, and set the company theme of using a large, lightly-stressed engine in strong cycle parts. It worked well and suited the American needs to cope with great distances and few paved roads.

In 1912 the V-twin engine capacity became 61ci (cubic inches) and there was a clutch, chain drive for most models, and a new frame that lowered the saddle and suspended it on a spring in the seat tube. Comfort was much improved. The singles grew for 1913 to become the 5-35, indicating 5hp and 35ci. At the same time they adopted the mechanical inlet valve while the range was joined by a forecar. This replaced the front forks with twin wheels with a trade box between them.

Two speeds, a sidecar, a drum rear brake and some racing were the key developments in 1914, while the next year brought a three-speed gearbox to complete the basic machine. From then on it would be refined and developed in changing times. While a war raged in Europe, the American motorcycle industry was shrinking from some 80-plus makes to Harley-Davidson, Indian and Excelsior. Their problem was Henry Ford and his Model T which led to a smaller market, hence the racing to seduce buyers into the sales room.

Harley-Davidson tried this route up to 1921, running a highly successful team known as the 'Wrecking Crew' who used both tuned F-head and 8-valve engines. The latter, supposedly production units for sale, were priced way out of reach and run by the team to break the opposition. Between six and ten engines are thought to have been built, along with some four-valve singles. They dominated for six years, but were dropped when the effect on sales seemed negligible.

Before then, in 1917, there was a change of colour to olive, and then the supply of 20,000 machines to the services. After the Great War the singles were dropped, but

**The 1911 V-twin model 7D which was priced at $300 and equipped with magneto ignition and 28-inch wheels.**

**Top: The model 7A single of 1911 when it sold for $250 when fitted with the magneto ignition.**

**Below: A fully restored 1915 twin in the colour that earned the machines the name of 'Silent Gray Fellow'.**

were to reappear from time to time, while the V-twins were joined by an oddball for 1919, the Sports Twin, which had a 35ci flat-twin engine. The cylinders of the side-valve motor lay fore and aft, the three-speed gearbox was built in unit above the crankcase, the rear chain was fully enclosed and trailing-link front forks were fitted. It was a clever move forward but not successful, being slower than the Indian Scout and only $15 cheaper than a Ford, so it was dropped after 1923

Sidecars were no problem for a Harley to haul along. This one is in France during the Great War.

Above: In contrast, this is the front cover of the 1915 catalogue which shows a wartime aspect before the USA became involved in the conflict.

Left: Pastoral advert of 1915; proceeds from the sale of copies went to provide food parcels for prisoners of war.

The model 16F twin with 7-9hp V-twin engine and three-speed gearbox as offered for 1916.

Below: Model 16C 4hp single for 1916 with magneto ignition and the three speeds.

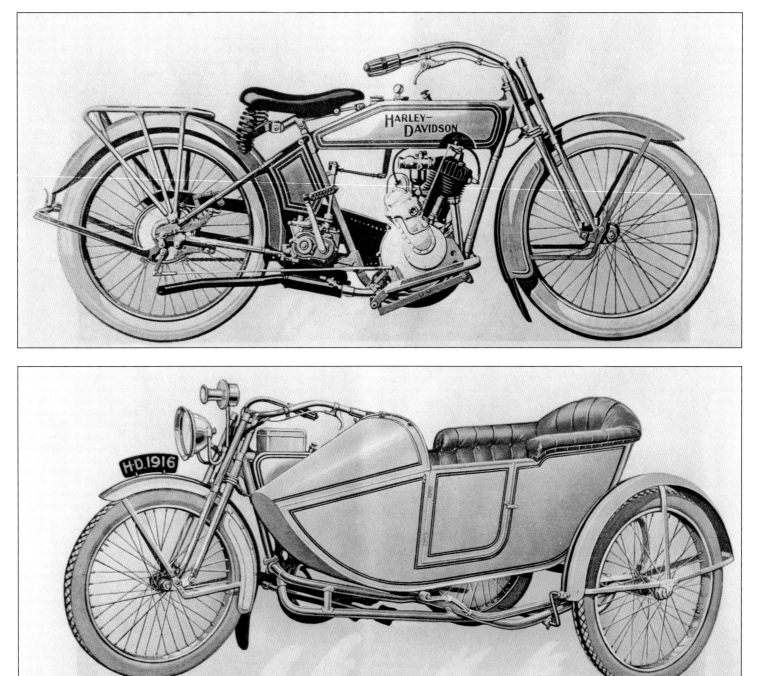

One of several sidecars offered by the firm in 1916, this one for the UK market, hence the leftside fitting.

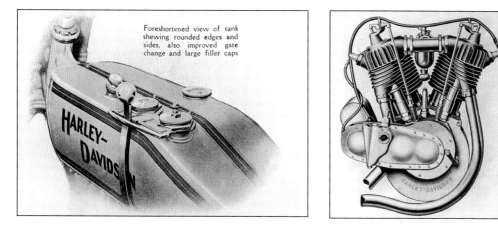

Foreshortened view of tank shewing rounded edges and sides, also improved gate change and large filler caps

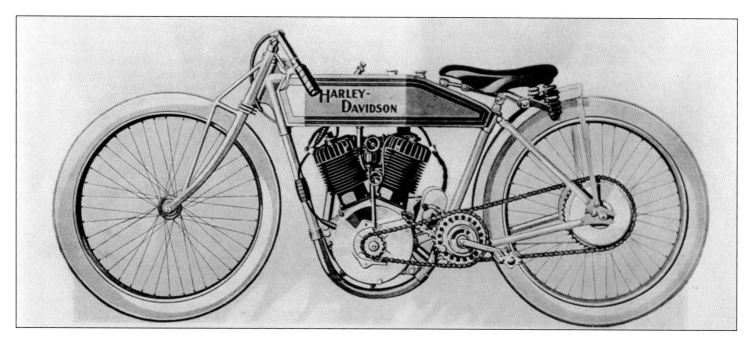

Far left: Tank top for 1916 with petrol on the right, oil to the left along with the gear change lever in its gate.

Left: The V-twin engine with its overhead inlet and side exhaust valves, an arrangement the firm used for many years.

Stripped model 16K which had a single speed and rigid forks, but two brakes in the rear hub.
A kit to enable the model to be used on the road was an option.

The short-lived, flat-twin model WA built from 1919 to 1923 as the 35 Sport.

# BIG TWIN

**S**uccess followed the addition of a 74ci model to the range for 1921, both this and the existing 61 being sold as F models with a magneto, and J models with a generator. The 74 was the easy route to more power for solo speed or sidecar hauling and was to be around for a long time. A commercial 37ci single, a 74 minus one cylinder, was listed for two years.

Seat heights went down for 1925 thanks to a new frame, and late that year a 21ci racing class was initiated, for which Harley-Davidson built an ohv single known as the Peashooter. Road versions of this with side- or overhead-valve engines were introduced in 1926. Many of these were exported, and the side-valve one was stretched out to 30.5ci for 1930. By then the smaller model was export only and not listed for 1931. It returned in side-valve form for 1932, the two sizes of machine continuing until 1934. An ohv 30.5 prototype was built in 1930 and led to a limited number of competition singles during the next few years.

Meanwhile, a front brake was introduced in 1928, a feature deemed unnecessary on unpaved roads, hence its late appearance, and dual headlights for 1929, the final year of the F-head models. They had survived since the firm began, but times demanded something different and Harley-Davidson survived by listening. Other firms were technically clever, but unskilled in keeping both customer and dealer happy and loyal. So new models were created for the next decade.

New, but still V-twins and reverting to side valves so apparently less efficient. However, this layout was quieter, cleaner, more reliable and did not drop valves into cylinders. Performance was no problem, for the side valve motor could run well enough, had a wide power band and was made large enough to give the power asked for by its American rider.

**Sports sidecar fitted with a disc wheel to match the motorcycle in 1921.**

Douglas Davidson on his Harley sidecar at Brooklands in 1921.
In April that year he rode a solo Harley to become the first officially to exceed IOOmph in England.

**Right: Meanwhile, the big twins ran on: this is the 1921 model with electric equipment.**

**Right: A two-seater sidecar with a hood and two screens attached to a 1924 74ci model JD twin for use in the UK.**

**Below: The 1924 model JE Super Speed version was built for the fast riders of the day but used the 61ci engine.**

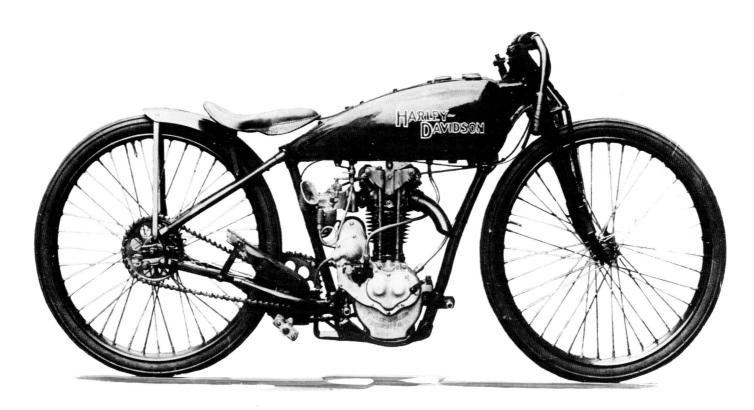

Peashooter 21ci racer first seen late in 1925 and built in flat track form as here, or with front suspension for US-type TT/road races.

This is the Parcelcar, a commercial sidecar type sold by Harley for many years and suited to its time; a 1926 or 1927 machine.

This is the 1928 version of the 21ci ohv single, hence the front brake, which was introduced that year.

Brochure picture of a 1927 model J which had the full electrics.

The 1928 74ci V-twin model which was nearing the end of its life.

Taken from the 1928 brochure, this shows both solo and sidecar Harley-Davidson out on the American roads of the time.

The 21ci side-valve single as for 1928.

Twin headlights were fitted for 1929; this model is the 74ci Two Cam version of the twin.

# SIDE-VALVE TWINS

The first new model with side valves was the Forty-five, which was basic but destined for a long life. Its capacity was 45ci, it had coil ignition and total-loss oiling, while transmission was by chain and three-speed gearbox, and suspension by leading-link forks and saddle. Listed as the model D, it was soon also available as the hotter DL, the sidecar DS and then the sports DLD.

The second new model was introduced late in 1929 and ran straight into all manner of technical problems - as if the Wall Street crash was not enough. It was a side-valve Seventy-four - although to a casual glance it might have appeared like a bulkier Forty-five, as it had a similar outline specification - and it was listed as the model V. It owed little to the old F-head engine, and it was offered in stock or hotter VL form, with the option of a magneto as the VM or VLM.

The firm worked fast to clear the problems and for a while all seemed well, but then the depression hit and sales dropped, falling to a 1933 low, little above the 1910 figure. It was a desperate period and every effort was made to drum up sales. One route was police business, another to introduce the Servi-Car. Based on the Forty-five, this had a tricycle layout of two rear wheels and was used to collect cars. It was hitched by tow bar to the car, which then hauled it back to the garage. It was to stay in production into the 1970s and became much used by traffic police.

Wage cuts and lay-offs became common as the firm set up a deal for their machines to be built under licence in Japan. This led to the sale of tools, dies and engineering know-how and created the Rikuo. More revenue was generated by the sale of Harley-Davidson clothing and accessories, something that continues to this day on a large scale.

During 1928 Harley launched the 45 as the model D, first of their side-valve twins. This is the 1930 version.

The Forty-five became the model R for 1932 and the popular Buddy Seat joined the option list the next year. Changes were minimal during this period, although evolution continued. A competition Forty-five was added for 1935 to suit the Class C racing set up to reduce costs by using stock machines. It was to serve the surviving American firms well for many years and Harley-Davidson offered a tuned Forty-five, complete with road equipment.

Late in 1935 things began to move once more. A larger V model made its debut - the Eighty, offering more capacity from a longer stroke. It was an easy way to add performance and the result was a 100mph machine that handled both corners and dirt or gravel roads well. There was a four-speed option even if the machine's design was dated.

**Right: A picture of a 45 taken from the 1930 brochure.**

**Below: The model V with a 74ci side-valve twin engine was introduced late in 1929, this being the 1930 brochure picture.**

Above: The Servi-Car, based on the 45, was a long-running Harley model, used here to collect or deliver cars for service, in this case a V-16 Cadillac.

Left: For parcels, the Package Truck continued to offer a cheap and efficient method of local delivery.

Stretched out to 30.5ci, or 500cc, for 1930, this side-valve single used the 45 cycle parts.

The 21ci side-valve single in its 1930 form.

Twin-port version of the 21ci ohv single as for 1930, still with the twin headlights.

Above: Brochure front cover for 1930 showing a neat outfit and the clothes style of the time.

Next page: *top left,* Front of the 1931 brochure, a year when selling anything really was tough.
*top right,* Front cover for 1932 kept the 45 as its lead machine, maybe because it was the one most people could afford.
*bottom,* The 1934 front cover and one determined looking rider.

THE SPORTY NEW 45 TWIN

Lines and colour of the model R 45 for 1934.
That long saddle tube contained the saddle spring which helped to make Harleys so comfortable for so long.

An early 1930s model V as restored and seen in the UK during 1993.

Right: The TNT 74ci engine as shown in the 1934 brochure, which gives a good view of its compact form.

Below: This is the look of both the 21 and 30.5ci singles for 1934, basic transport with side valves.

Bottom: The 1934 model V was offered with a special TNT engine as well as the stock one; in other respects the machines were the same.

Opposite: Brochure front cover for 1937 which featured a model U with 80ci engine.

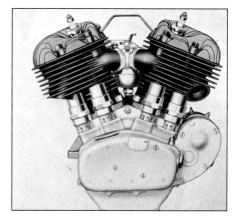

PRESENTATION OF

★ HARLEY -

# KNUCKLEHEAD

he major new model for 1936 was the 61 OHV, listed as the E series but soon known as the Knucklehead because of a detail of the engine styling. It had been under development since 1931 and was a radical move forward, having dry sump lubrication, a four-speed gearbox and great style that was both new and fresh. From its concept would develop the Harley-Davidson V-twins down the years.

To a large extent the 61 OHV followed factory convention, with the cylinders at 45 degrees, rigid frame, leading-link forks and footboards. But the frame was new, and also destined for the 74 and 80 models, the forks improved, tanks new and a magnificent tank-top instrument panel was flanked by the two fuel caps.

For the times, the Knucklehead was an act of faith, and the faithful responded. Despite some early hitches, sales that first year exceeded factory expectations. This enabled the firm to rationalise production for 1937 by using the frame, tank and wheels of the 61 OHV for the side-valve Seventy-four and Eighty models which became the U Series. Both went over to dry-sump lubrication, as did the Forty-five, this becoming the W Series, and Harley-Davidson continued to list a model for Class C races.

The four-model range ran on through the late 1930s and into 1940. While Europe went to war, the US Army discussed a variety of motorcycle proposals with its domestic manufacturers which led to the WLA model, a Forty-five built to suit their needs. An order followed in 1940, along with a contract for a batch of tricycles which used the 61 OHV engine.

For 1941 the firm introduced two new models, the 74 OHV and the WR. The first was derived from the 61 OHV, produced more power and was listed as the F series. The second was a pure Class C racing model, offered in road or flat-track form, and no longer kitted out with stock items. The WR was special, but basic and available, to be all things to all racers thanks to a long option list. Thus, the racing became

**Model E with 61ci Knucklehead engine as in 1937. Their first production ohv twin.**

61 TWIN
Right Side

more equal, tuning and riding abilities more important than just the money.

Then the USA was at war although the factory was already at work producing the WLA and a derivative, the WLC, for the Canadian forces. They also had a contract to develop and build a small batch of machines with flat-twin engines. The outcome was the XA, a copy of a 45ci, 750cc BMW with side valves, four speeds, plunger rear suspension and the desired shaft drive. A special version had a sidecar with its wheel driven, but the army settled for the Jeep.

**Top left:** The famous Knucklehead engine, 61ci or 1000cc, ohv and the forerunner of the modern types.

**Top right:** The instrument panel with speedometer, gauges and switch, flanked by petrol caps on each side.

**Below:** The timing side of the 1937 model U fitted with the 80ci engine, a huge 1340cc.

Drive side of the smaller 74ci model U of 1937.

The smallest 1937 twin was this 45ci model W which differed from the others in having its drive chain on the right.

A fine Knucklehead seen at Daytona in 1994, its label and finish indicating that it is a 1939 EL model.

Fully restored 1941 Knucklehead pictured recently.

**Right:** The WLA, as built for the services during World War II. Many of these machines were used by civilians postwar.

**Below:** Model UL police machine from 1941 in a more modern setting.

Above: This object is the siren for the 1941 police bike, well positioned for the errant car driver's right ear. Once stopped, even if deaf, you can read which state has pulled you over.

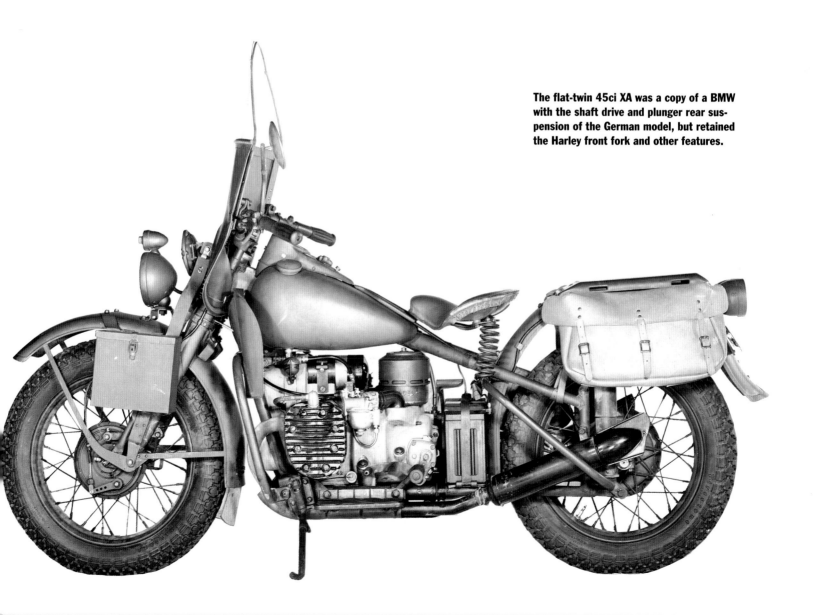

The flat-twin 45ci XA was a copy of a BMW with the shaft drive and plunger rear suspension of the German model, but retained the Harley front fork and other features.

# POSTWAR AND PANHEAD

When the war ended, Harley-Davidson was well placed to pick up where it had left off, building the prewar range minus the Eighty. The four-model range was joined late in 1947 by something completely new, a lightweight using a tiny 7.5ci two-stroke engine. This was really a war reparation job, a 1935 German DKW taken up by BSA as the Bantam, by Russia as the Voskhod, by DKW in the East German sector and by Yamaha as the YA1 or Red Dragonfly.

For 1951 telescopic front forks replaced the original girders, providing a Tele-Glide model name, while for 1953 the engine was stretched to 165cc. In 1955 the 125 returned, both models being known as the Hummer and offering basic fun and local transport. Their main problem was not being perceived as a real Harley-Davidson.

Back in 1948 the ohv V-twins continued their evolution in a move to light-alloy cylinder heads and hydraulic valve lifters. The change of rocker cover brought a new nickname, the Panhead, while the need for the old side-valve Seventy-Four diminished and it was dropped at the end of the year.

Telescopic front forks appeared on the ohv Panhead twins for 1949 when they were given the model name of Hydra-Glide, and in this form, along with the 125 and the venerable Forty-five, the range rolled along to 1952. That was to be the last year for the 61E, while the 45 was replaced by the same-size model K. This had a foot gearchange, telescopic front forks and pivoted-fork rear suspension. The foot change was also an option for the 74, although for that model the old hand method remained available. The K-series engine represented both old and new, for it kept the side valves of the 45 but had its four-speed gearbox built in unit with the engine.

The model K was not very fast, unlike the racing KR which was derived from it, and which remained in production until 1968. For the stock machine the engine was stretched out to 54ci in 1954. There was also a sports kit which further enhanced the performance, but the K, for all its up-to-date features, seemed to lack the essentials for success.

**After the war the V-twin range ran on and included the elderly 45, this the 1948 model.**

Wartime 45 engines were often used years later, married to another gearbox, fitted with teles and mildly customised to give a pleasing effect.

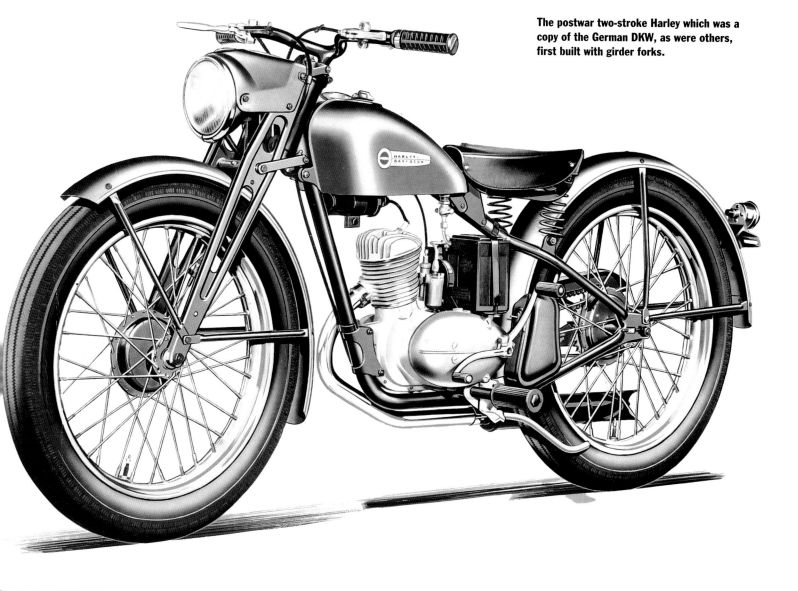

The postwar two-stroke Harley which was a copy of the German DKW, as were others, first built with girder forks.

The two-stroke was later known as the 'Hummer', built in 165cc as well as 125cc capacity, and fitted with teles in 1951 to become the Tele-Glide model.

Close-up of a Panhead engine showing the characteristic rocker box covers which gave rise to the name.

Many Harley-Davidson twins were used for police patrol work both in the USA and elsewhere,
like this one used by the Los Angeles force.

When telescopic front forks were adopted by the Panhead for 1949, the model name became Hydra-Glide.

Tail end of a later Shovelhead which was decked out with many detail extras.

Telescopic front forks and rigid rear of the same machine suggest a Hydra-Glide, but the engine is a later Shovelhead seen at Daytona in 1991.

Finely restored 1954 model KH, the flat-head with unit-construction, rear suspension and a hand clutch.

Racing version of the 45, possibly a WR model, working at a flat track event at which the model was most successful.

A KR racer set up for the dirt track, hence the rigid frame and other changes. Behind it stands an early Sportster drag racer with similar modifications.

# SPORTSTER AND DUO-GLIDE

**H**arley-Davidson had the answer to the model K's power problem already in development and in 1957 it was replaced by the XL Sportster, a success story. In essence it was a K fitted with overhead valves, but in the process the engine dimensions were altered to fatten the bore and shorten the stroke while keeping the 54ci capacity, the equivalent 883cc later appearing in the model code. More power, model variations and a long option list soon appeared, which resulted in few Sportsters leaving the factory alike.

Two versions were to predominate: first the touring XLH fitted with big tank, buddy seat, single exhaust and coil ignition; second the sports XLCH with small tank, single seat, dual pipes and a magneto. Alongside, the competition XLR model joined the KR - special, powerful and for non-championship events. It was listed until 1969 but then, to conform to a change in the rules, it was replaced by the XR-750 with iron engine. This was a rush job which proved too slow and fragile, but in 1972 the alloy XR750 was introduced, and the factory had a winning legend for the next two decades.

In 1958 the Panhead Seventy-four had rear suspension added to become the Duo-Glide, renamed the Electra Glide in 1965 when an electric starter was added. For 1966 the engine top end was revised to a new shape which led to the name Shovelhead. So the various Electra Glide models rolled on as large highway machines for some years, the Sportster following suit, with the electric start fitted to the touring models for 1968. During this time the factory offered a tour package, at first a fairing plus saddlebags, later a top box as well. They continued to list a sidecar and, to suit this limited market, offered an option of three speeds and reverse right up to the late 1970s. The Glide electrics changed for 1970, early models becoming Generator Shovels, later ones Alternator Shovels.

The XL Sportster series was launched in 1957 - in essence a K engine with ohv, but also altered - to create a long-running and popular series. This is a modified 1959 model.

**Above:** Typical of the stripped Sportster with the small tank and dual shorty pipes, this XLCH is from early 1965.

**Right:** Unusual use of a Sportster engine adapted for speedway by removing the rear cylinder.

After 1968 the XR750 took over the racing mantle for Harley-Davidson and became a dominant force. This is an early flat track version with the iron engine.

The XR750 in its iron engine form.

A Duo-Glide seen at the BMF rally in 1993, a very good example of the type.

Engine close-up of the Duo-Glide to show the Panhead engine detail.

Matching buddies move off for the parade to Daytona circuit in 1991, typical of the Harley owner who adds touring extras.

Brands Hatch in 1986 and a smart police Servi-Car which combined the 45 engine and the Hydra-Glide front forks.

Above: Another touring Harley seen in Main Street, Daytona, in 1991.

Main Street, Daytona, and this Harley is well fitted out with touring and personal extras.

Stock FL Electra Glide for 1975, fitted with the screen, panniers and long seat for the tourer.

Not all custom machines were built in the USA. This one is seen at the 1993 BMF Rally and represents a great deal of work.

Above: Sidecars continued to be listed for the Harley twin, usually hitched to an Electra Glide as here.

Some owners did go over the top, hauling a sidecar and trailer with a paddock bike on the trailer lid. Daytona 1991 parade to the circuit.

# FOREIGN LINKS AND AMF

In 1960, outside events affected the firm and introduced models very different from the traditional Harley-Davidson V-twin. That year the firm linked up with Aermacchi in Italy and began importing their 250cc four-stroke singles in various forms. Alongside these, the Hummer was updated as the Super 10 and then the Ranger, Pacer and Scat, all dropped by 1965 as Italian imports took their place. There were 50 and 65cc models, the 125cc Rapido, 100cc Baja and 175cc Bobcat. There was even a scooter, the Topper.

Aermacchi SS350 from 1973, its engine typical of the Italian singles.

Late Aermacchi Sprint with one-piece rocker cover which changed the engine lines. The more usual one is behind.

On the commercial side, the families sold shares in 1965 to raise capital and then, in 1969, the firm was bought by American Machine Foundry, a large conglomerate known as AMF. They put in money and made changes, moved assembly to York in Pennsylvania, and ran into quality problems as production boomed in the first half of the 1970s.

Via the Italian connection, the 250 single was joined by a 350 in 1969, fine motorcycles at home, but less suited to the US market. Around 1973 they were replaced by a

The off-road 100cc Baja was Italian in origin, even if the name came from the famous Mexican race.

Below: One of the range of Italian two-strokes which the firm sold for a few short years.

two-stroke line which was average and then in 1978 AMF sold off Aermacchi to Cagiva to end the Italian link. Along the way there were racing versions of the 250 single and the RR250, a road racing model fitted with a watercooled, twin-cylinder two-stroke engine. Factory versions won the 250cc world title in 1974, 1975 and 1976, also taking the 350cc title in that last year.

While 1970 was the year when the Electra Glide went to an alternator, 1971 brought a new line, the Super Glide or FX. This took the Seventy-four alternator engine, the Glide frame and rear suspension, but fitted the Sportster forks and front wheel. There was no electric start and the rear fender and seat base were in a fibre-glass moulding known as the Boatback. This was not a popular fitting so was dropped after the first year, but the model had style, speed and handling while Harley-Davidson had a new line.

The early 1970s brought disc front brakes and 1972 a larger, 1000cc engine for the Sportsters. Electric start became an option for the 1974 Super Glide while 1975 saw the Sportster gear lever move to the left to obey federal rules. Added models for 1977 were the Low Rider FXS in chopper style with low seat, raked forks, cast wheels and tank top instrument panel. It was another step forward for the company. That same year brought a touring Sportster, the XLT, and the XLCR, a Café Racer version, but neither sold well. However, the XLCR had a new frame and in 1978 it was adopted for the Sportster range which went over to electronic ignition, as did the Electra Glide which also changed its engine size to 82ci, or 1340cc.

The final year of the l970s saw the Super Glide range get the electronic ignition plus a new model called the Fat Bob, which was a Low Rider with a fat fuel tank and short fenders. During the year, the 82ci engine became a range option. A low rider format was used for a new Sportster, the XLS, which sold well, while the Electra Glide was joined by the CLE, a sidecar machine, and the Tour Glide. This last was a major step forward, as the engine and gearbox were bolted together as one, had the rear fork pivoted to the assembly, and had this attached via isolating mounts to a

**Road models were listed with engines from 125 to 250cc, all similar in style. This is just one of the series.**

new frame. And there were five speeds in the gearbox plus an enclosed rear chain.

The first year of the 1980s saw yet more Super Glide models, the first the Wide Glide created from the Fat Bob by widening the front forks, fitting the 82ci engine and using a 21 inch front wheel to produce a factory chopper. The second was the Sturgis, a Low Rider with the bigger engine and belts for both primary and final drives. For all the Glides it was the last year for the 74ci engine. In the Sportster range there were two models, the XLS Roadster and the XLH Hugger with lower seat level.

Major events occurred during 1981, for AMF realised that making motorcycles that sold was a tricky business indeed. They had invested heavily in facilities, less so in new product and these decisions began to have a detrimental effect. So a group formed of members of the families, employees, and AMF personnel borrowed from banks and bought Harley-Davidson from AMF. It changed many things.

**Many 250 and 350cc Aermacchi race machines had a further lease of life in classic racing where they continued to be successful.**

**One of the range of off-road two-strokes from Italy which was soon sold on to Cagiva.**

The factory raced two-stroke twins at grand prix level for several years, Walter Villa taking the 250 title for 1974-76 and the 350 one in the last year.

The Super Glide first appeared in 1971 by combining parts from the Electra Glide and Sportster ranges, this being a 1975 FX1200

Sportster XLCH from 1974, when the
engine had grown to 1000cc but the gear
lever was still on the right.

An Electra Glide FLH from 1975 when it
managed with the 1200 engine, even if the
owner added more extras.

The Super Glide 1200 in its late-1970s form when offered with kick FX or electric FXE start.

The Low Rider FXS was a new style for 1977 with low seat and other custom features, this being a 1978 version.

The XLT touring Sportster was introduced for 1977 and proved a popular model.

Below: Café racer style Sportster, the XLCR 1000 of 1977 which failed to attract the buyers.

Electra Glide for 1978 when it was still the FLH-1200.

Below: For 1978 Harley-Davidson offered an Anniversary Sportster to celebrate its 75th year of business, but this one is from 1982.

Above: For 1978 the Electra Glide was fitted with the 82-inch engine.

Right: Typical of the high standard of work and the time and effort that owners would put into creating their own concept of a Harley. Main Street, Daytona, 1991.

Super Glide FXE in its 1981 form.

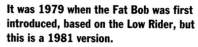

It was 1979 when the Fat Bob was first introduced, based on the Low Rider, but this is a 1981 version.

The Sportster XLS was introduced for 1979 with an exhaust system based on that of the café racer.

**Right:** The Tour Glide Classic with sidecar was still offered in the 1980s to continue a long running listing.

**Below:** The FLT Tour Glide was added to the list for 1979 and offered several major improvements.

The Wide Glide descended from the Fat Bob, itself a Low Rider derivative of a Super Glide. This is a typical example seen in 1994.

The Wide Glide was sold in Flame as well as Plain finish for 1981.

Right: Custom builders soon had their own ideas as to what made a Wide Glide, this one parked in Main Street, Daytona, in 1991.

Below: This was an English version of a custom Wide Glide seen at the BMF Rally in 1993. Lots of work.

The XSL Sportster was named the Roadster for 1980 following its 1979 introduction.

Below: The Huger XLH Sportster was another new model for 1980, its name derived from its lowered seat.

# FXR AND EVOLUTION

A new series appeared for 1982, the FXR, listed for a while as Super Glide II but really hardly related to either the Electra or Super Glides. The models, with wire or cast wheels, used the 82ci engine, five-speed gearbox, isolating mounts and a new frame. It was a better motorcycle and popular, so Harley-Davidson had another line. The old continued with Super Glides in stock, Low Rider, Wide Glide and Sturgis forms, the Electra Glide the classic tourer, and the Sportsters in a new frame.

For 1983 the FXR series added the Sport Glide, really a tourer, and the Sportsters added two models. One, the XLX-61, was the simplest that the firm could build, a real budget model which pulled the customers into the showroom, sold them, and then added the options. The other was the XR-1000, a fast race-styled model fitted with the alloy heads from the XR-750, dual carbs and left-side exhausts. It was priced high at $2000 over the XLH, but looked too much like the XLX to sell well.

Meanwhile, a new all-alloy engine, the V2 Evolution, appeared during 1984. Along with a diaphragm clutch and still of 82ci, it went into the Electra Glide, the three FXR models and a new Super Glide. The Electra Glide had air-assisted rear shocks and anti-dive front forks, while the FXR machines were the touring Sports Glide, a reduced height Low Glide and the Disc Glide, which was the Low plus a solid rear wheel.

The new machine in the FX series was the Softail. Essentially a Wide Glide, it had the rear part of the frame styled to appear rigid, and to aid this the suspension

**The FXRS Super Glide II of 1982 was the deluxe form of the model fitted with cast wheels.**

FXE Super Glide for the early
1980s, after the AMF days.

springs went under the engine. The four-speed gearbox was used along with a
21 inch front wheel and a stepped seat. It came along just as the market swung to
the retro-style and buyers sought the old to be in fashion. Only Harley-Davidson
could build and sell such a machine. The copyists failed, and enthusiasts explained
that the riding posture was all wrong, but it sold in droves - to the buyers seeking
'the look'. Those planning to ride coast-to-coast bought the Electra Glide or an air-
plane ticket.

The diaphragm clutch and an alternator went into the Sportsters during the year,
and these ran on for 1985 minus the XR-1000 Café Racer. That year brought belt
final drive for the FL series and the FXR models and the Evolution engine for the
rest of the Super Glides along with the diaphram clutch and belt drive for the Low
Rider and Wide Glide.

In 1986 the Fat Bob and Low Rider were dropped, the Low Glide became the Low
Rider, a Custom version of the Softail was added using the five-speed gearbox and
belt final drive, so only the Wide Glide was left with four speeds. There was a Sport
Edition of the Low Rider listed as the FXRS-SP and a Sport Glide Grand Tourer as
the FXRD. The FL series had a round air cleaner and from then on continued little
altered, offering the best in touring, often plus a sidecar and a trailer as well.

For the Sportster line 1986 brought a radical new engine which could still trace its
ancestry but took the model a long step forward. The concept stayed but the
engine was all-alloy and came in two sizes to create the XLH-883 and the XLH-1100
by means of larger bores and valves. Otherwise they were the same, with hydraulic
valve lifters, the diaphragm clutch, an alternator and four speeds. The XLX frame
and running gear housed the new engines and there were soon lots of options. It
was another success story, joined by a lower built Hugger 883 model for 1987.

A Low Rider Custom was added to the FXR series for 1987, using 21 inch front and
solid disc rear wheels to create another machine with the cool look. The Heritage
Softail appeared that year to combine the rigid-frame look with something of the
Glide series of the past. For 1988 the big Sportster was opened up to become the
XLH-1200 and revive memories of the old 74 even if that number was not used.

The Low Rider FXS as for 1982
when Harley was once more

FXS Low Rider

Below: Wide Glide FXWG model for
the 1982-83 period, after AMF and
before the Evo engine arrived.

FXWG Wideglide

Above: The FLHC Electra glide Classic was simply more of the same, sold with more extras as stock.

FLTC Tour Glide Classic

Left: When fitted out with the basics for long-distance travel - fairing, top box, panniers and radio, the tourer was listed as the FLTC Tour Glide Classic.

Sport Glide FXRT introduced for 1983 but really a touring model.

The 1983 budget XLX-61 Sportster was built to pull customers into the showrooms and this it did.

The high-priced XR-1000 of 1983 which had alloy heads and other race-oriented features to push the price up further than the model's looks would stand.

For 1984 the Electra Glide was fitted with the V2 Evolution engine, a major step forward.

Third in the FXR series to fit the new engine was this FXRDG Disc Glide model which had a solid rear wheel.

New for 1984 was the Softail, listed as the FXST, with rear suspension but the looks of a rigid frame.

Sportster XLH for 1984, the year the clutch and electrics were revised.

Tour Glide Classic FLTC fitted with the new Evolution engine for 1984.

Low Rider FXSB was another model fitted with belt drive by 1984.

The sport edition of the Low Rider was listed as the FXRS-SP, this one on test in England.

Left: A police version of the FXRT Sport Glide doing duty in the UK for a change.

Below: This 1987 FLHTC Electra Glide Ultra Classic demonstrates the very full equipment level offered by the factory to those who wanted it.

Right: Typical owner of an Electra Glide riding down Main Street, Daytona, during race week, 1991.

Below: Ultra Classic Electra Glide, the ultimate tourer, in its 1994 form, having changed little over the years.

The Sportster was revised with a new, all-alloy engine for 1986. The smaller was listed as the XLH-883. This is the 1989 version.

The FXLR Low Rider Custom model joined the range for 1987, featuring large wire front and small solid rear wheels.

Heritage Softail FLST which combined the looks of the past with the modern Harley rear suspension.

A Sportster from the late-1980s, with more chrome plating added by the owner.

# SPRINGER RETURN

**M**ajor 1988 news was the Springer, a Super Glide variant that took the Softail and moved it further back into the past by fitting leading-link front forks based on those seen on the early Harley but revised using modern aids. It also had the solid engine mounts, five speeds and the hidden rear shocks. A Classic version of the Heritage Softail joined the line along with a Sport Edition of the Electra Glide.

For 1989 there was the Low Rider Convertible, a basic FXR whose saddlebags and screen had quick-release fasteners to switch easily from sports to touring. Ultra Classic versions of the Electra and Tour Glides were added to the range, and these had more extras as standard. The Fat Boy version of the Super Glide was introduced for 1990, a Softail with solid disc wheels front and rear and gray paint to effect a different, solid look which soon found its market niche.

The Sturgis returned in the FXR line for 1991 to introduce a new frame and isolating mounting system, known as Dyna Glide, and using the Evolution engine, five-speed gearbox, belt final drive and cast wheels to make a good package. The same year brought five speeds for the Sportster along with belt final drive for the 1200 and Deluxe 883.

The Daytona replaced the Sturgis for 1992 gaining a second front disc, buckhorn bars and a brighter paint job. Alongside it came the Dyna Glide Custom using the same mechanics, while the rest of the FXR models continued. All four Sportsters ran on, as did the remaining models, with the exception of the Tour Glide Classic, although the Ultra version of this continued.

**A return to the past in 1988, when the FXSTS Springer was introduced with the old-style front forks brought up to date.**

Above: Heritage Softail Special FLST on
show in 1989 - a fine example of
Harley-Davidson style and fitments.

Right: This is the 1991 version of the Low
Rider Convertible in its touring form with
the panniers and screen in place.

The Ultra Classic version of the Electra Glide as for 1989.

Tour Glide Ultra Classic FLTC as for 1992, carrying even more extras as standard.

Above: This Fat Boy version of the Super Glide, listed as the FLSTF, was introduced for 1990.

Right: The Sturgis FXDB which was only listed for 1991, but was fitted with the new Dyna Glide frame.

**Police business was a Harley stand-by for many, many years. This one has pulled you over in 1991.**

Near stock, simply adapted to suit its police work.

Daytona FXDB model from 1992, a Sturgis plus second front
disc and other detail changes.

The Dyna Glide Custom FXDC of 1992.

Hugger version of the XLH Sportster model with reduced seat height.

During 1992, one AA patrolman turned to this Electra Glide for his duties out on the roads.
Based on the Californian police machines, it worked well.

A 1994 Sportster 1200 plus accessories.

Electra Glide Classic **FLHTC** for 1994, a touring model for long, long distances.

Glide plus sidecar, still popular with a number of owners and sometimes seen towing a trailer as well.

Main street Daytona, and a typical shop during race week with a fine line of tee-shirts.

On the morning of the 200-mile race, a parade runs from this shopping mall to the track, most of the vast crowd riding Harleys.

Lovely graphic of an early model on the side of Bud's Bike shack in Austin, Texas.

Below: Inside Bud's Bike shack are all these machines and spares waiting for customers to choose.

# 90TH ANNIVERSARY

For 1993 the standard Sportster went over to belt final drive, the XLH-1200 was listed as an Anniversary model, and the Electra and Tour Glides ran on in stock and Anniversary forms.

These Anniversary versions were there to celebrate the 90 years that Harley-Davidson had been in the business of building motorcycles, a very long time indeed. This theme continued in the FXR and Super Glide ranges, the first of these adding the Dyna Low Rider in place of the Daytona Custom model, while retaining the basic Super Glide and Low Riders in Custom, Convertible and Sports forms.

In the FX Glide series the Springer, Softail Custom, Fat Boy and Heritage Softail were joined by two further models. These were a Nostalgia version of the Heritage and the Dyna Wide Glide to mark the return of a former model style.

Harley-Davidson rolled on into 1994 and its 91st year with most of the existing range. The De Luxe 883 Sportster was dropped but the other three ran on as entry-level models, as did the FX Glide series of machines. In the FXR range the Super Glide, Dyna Low Rider and Low Rider Custom continued but the Low Rider Sport was dropped and the Convertible went into the Dyna frame. Finally, the Electra Glide Road King joined the touring range which comprised the Electra Glide Classic and the Ultra Classic Electra Glide, both complete with fairing, panniers and top box.

Thus, the Harley-Davidson legend rumbles on, the 45 degree V-twin emitting that special, off-beat, but so distinctive note. Style, line and form have changed since 1911, not the sound of a Harley twin at tickover.

Very special, so, as the legend says, 'live to ride – ride to live'.

**The Anniversary edition of the Ultra Classic Tour Glide which celebrated 90 years of motorcycle production in 1993.**

Dyna Low Rider model introduced for 1993, the firm's 90th year.

Fine 1989 FXR which has had some discreet changes to its front fender, tank and paint colour but most of the parts are listed in the extensive option list.

The 1994 Low Rider Custom FXLR model.

A FXDS-CONV Dyna Low Rider Convertible for 1994, here fitted with its screen and panniers.

The 1994 Springer Softail with its old-style frame and forks updated with modern techniques.

Softail Custom model FXSTC for 1994 from the Super Glide series.

The 1994 Fat Boy with its Softail rear suspension system and solid disc wheels.

Heritage Softail Classic model with old-style tank colour and decals matching the line of frame and forks.

The Dyna Wide Glide model returned for 1993 as the FXDWG, this the 1994 version.

One of the many race Sportsters at Daytona in 1994.

Grid line up for the 1994 Sportster race at Daytona.

Just as always, owners attending the 1994 Daytona race week rode their fancy.

Harley ran this race replica VR1000 in the 1994 Daytona 200-mile race, buyers queuing up to buy the production machines. The engine was an eight-valve, V-twin, just as in 1916, but watercooled and with the cylinders at 60 degrees.

Instrument panels from two eras, on the left that from the early 1950s, on the right from 40 years later.

Below: Archetypal Harley-Davidson, the big V-twin tourer they have built since 1911, always powerful enough to haul all the luggage anyone would want. But only one of the many styles offered by the firm.

# HARLEY-DAVIDSON
# MODEL LIST

Harley-Davidson have used a complex variety of names, numbers and letters to distinguish series, models, engines, capacities and machine types. Today differs from the early times and the system needs practice to follow. The major lines only are shown here.

**Willie G. Davidson (the man) with Peter de Savary on the pillion.**

## Engine types

| Type | Years | Capacities |
|---|---|---|
| **V-twins** | | |
| F-head | 1909 – 29 | 50, 61, 74 cu. in. |
| 8 -valve | 1916 – 22 | 61 cu. in. |
| Flathead | 1928 – 74 | 45, 55, 74, 80 cu. in. |
| Knucklehead | 1936 – 47 | 61, 74 cu. in. |
| Panhead | 1948 – 65 | 61, 74 cu. in. |
| Shovelhead | 1966 – 84 | 74, 80 cu. in. |
| Evolution | 1984 – date | 80 cu. in. |
| Sportster | 1957 – 85 | 55, 61 cu. in. |
| Evo Sportster | 1986 – date | 883, 1100, 1200cc |
| VR1000 | 1994 | 1000cc |
| **Singles** | | |
| F-head | 1903 – 23 | 25, 30, 35, 37 cu. in. |
| 4-valve | 1916 – 22 | 30 cu. in. |
| Flathead | 1926 – 34 | 21, 30 cu. in. |
| OHV | 1926 – 37 | 21, 30 cu. in. |
| **Flat twins** | | |
| Flathead | 1919 – 23 | 36 cu. in. |
| Flathead | 1941 – 44 | 45 cu. in. |

## Chassis

| Name | Year | Engines |
|---|---|---|
| Hydra-Glide | 1949 – 57 | 61, 74 cu. in. |
| Tele-Glide | 1951 – 59 | 125, 165 cc |
| Duo-Glide | 1958 – 64 | 74 cu. in. |
| Electra Glide | 1965 – date | 74, 80 cu. in. |
| Tour Glide | 1980 – date | 80 cu. in. |
| Dyna Glide | 1991 – date | 80 cu. in. |

| Model code | Model name | Years | Capacities |
|---|---|---|---|
| **Sportsters** | | | |
| XL, XLH, XLCH | Sportster | 1957 – 71 | 55 cu. in. |
| XLH, XLCH | Sportster | 1972 – 85 | 61 cu. in. |
| XLT | Tourer | 1977 – 78 | 61 cu. in. |
| XLCR | Café Racer | 1977 – 78 | 61 cu. in. |
| XLS | Roadster | 1979 – 85 | 61 cu. in. |
| XLH | Hugger | 1980 – 85 | 61 cu. in. |
| XLX-61 | Sportster | 1983 – 85 | 61 cu. in. |
| XR1000 | Café Racer | 1983 – 84 | 61 cu. in. |
| XLH | Evo Sportster | 1986 – date | 883, 1100, 1200cc |
| XLH | Hugger | 1987 - date | 883cc |

| Type | | Years | Capacities |
|---|---|---|---|
| **Glides** | | | |
| FL, FLH | Electra Glide | 1965 – date | 74, 80 cu. in. |
| FLT | Tour Glide | 1979 – 92 | 80 cu. in. |
| FLHS | Electra Glide Sport | 1988 – 93 | 80 cu. in. |
| FLHTC | Ultra Classic | 1989 – date | 80 cu. in. |
| FLTC | Ultra Classic Tour | 1989 – 93 | 80 cu. in. |
| FLHR | Road King | 1994 - date | 80 cu. in. |
| | | | |
| **Super Glides** | | | |
| FX, FXE | Super Glide | 1971 – 84 | 74, 80 cu. in. |
| FXS, FXSB | Low Rider | 1977 – 85 | 74, 80 cu. in. |
| FXEF | Fat Bob | 1979 – 82 | 74,  80 cu. in. |
| FXWG | Wide Glide | 1980 – 85 | 80 cu. in. |
| FXB | Sturgis | 1980 – 82 | 80 cu. in. |
| FXST | Softail | 1984 – 90 | 80 cu. in. |
| FXEF | Fat Bob | 1985 | 80 cu. in. |
| FXSTC | Softail Custom | 1986 – date | 80 cu. in. |
| FLST | Heritage Softail | 1987 – 90 | 80 cu. in. |
| FLSTC | Heritage Classic | 1988 – date | 80 cu. in. |
| FXSTS | Springer Softail | 1988 – date | 80 cu. in. |
| FLSTF | Fat Boy | 1990 – date | 80 cu. in. |
| FXDWG | Dyna Wide Glide | 1993 – date | 80 cu. in. |
| FLSTN | Heritage Nostalgia | 1933 – date | 80 cu. in. |
| | | | |
| **FXR Series** | | | |
| FXR | Super Glide II | 1982 – 83 | 80 cu. in. |
| FXRT | Sport Glide | 1983 – 92 | 80 cu. in. |
| FXRDG | Disc Glide | 1984 | 80 cu. in. |
| FXRS | Low Glide | 1984 – 85 | 80 cu. in. |
| FXRC | Low Glide Custom | 1985 | 80 cu. in. |
| FXRS | Low Rider | 1986 – date | 80 cu. in. |
| FXRS – SP | Low Rider Sport | 1986 – 93 | 80 cu. in. |
| FXRD | Sport Glide Tourer | 1986 | 80 cu. in. |
| FXR | Super Glide | 1986 – date | 80 cu. in. |
| FXLR | Low Rider Custom | 1987 – date | 80 cu. in. |
| FXRS – CONV | Low Rider Conv | 1989 – date | 80 cu. in. |
| FXDB | Sturgis | 1991 | 80 cu. in. |
| FXDB | Daytona | 1992 | 80 cu. in. |
| FXDC | Dyna Glide Custom | 1992 | 80 cu. in. |
| FXDL | Dyna Low Rider | 1993 – date | 80 cu. in. |
| FXDS – CONV | Dyna Low Rider Conv | 1994 - date | 80 cu. in. |
| | | | |
| **Small singles** | | | |
| | Hummer | 1947 – 59 | 125, 165cc |
| | Super 10 | 1960 – 61 | 165 cc |
| | Topper | 1960 – 65 | 165 cc |
| | Ranger | 1962 | 165 cc |
| | Scat | 1962 – 65 | 175 cc |
| | Pacer | 1962 – 65 | 175 cc |
| | Bobcat | 1966 | 175 cc |
| | | | |
| **Imports** | | | |
| | Sprint | 1961 – 74 | 250, 350 cc |
| | Leggero | 1965 – 72 | 50, 65 cc |
| | Rapido | 1968 – 72 | 125 cc |
| | Baja 100 | 1970 – 72 | 100 cc |
| | Two-strokes | 1973 – 77 | 90, 125, 175, 250 cc |